A View from Heaven

CAROLYN NEARY
Dr. Paul Day

Copyright © 2017 Carolyn Neary & Dr. Paul Day.

Interior Graphics Credit: Linda Lee

Music Credit: Jon Day

All rights reserved. No part of this book may be used or reproduced by any means, graphic, electronic, or mechanical, including photocopying, recording, taping or by any information storage retrieval system without the written permission of the author except in the case of brief quotations embodied in critical articles and reviews.

WestBow Press books may be ordered through booksellers or by contacting:

WestBow Press
A Division of Thomas Nelson & Zondervan
1663 Liberty Drive
Bloomington, IN 47403
www.westbowpress.com
1 (866) 928-1240

Because of the dynamic nature of the Internet, any web addresses or links contained in this book may have changed since publication and may no longer be valid. The views expressed in this work are solely those of the author and do not necessarily reflect the views of the publisher, and the publisher hereby disclaims any responsibility for them.

Any people depicted in stock imagery provided by Thinkstock are models, and such images are being used for illustrative purposes only.
Certain stock imagery © Thinkstock.

ISBN: 978-1-5127-7065-0 (sc)
ISBN: 978-1-5127-7064-3 (e)

Library of Congress Control Number: 2017900079

Print information available on the last page.

WestBow Press rev. date: 03/28/2017

Endorsements

We thank God for Carolyn Neary and the gift she is to the body of Christ! She has an anointing to hear from heaven and to release the word of the Lord that brings churches together and sets the people free! You will want to purchase this beautiful devotional that describes her many heavenly downloads and visitations. Each section is prefaced with the exquisite artwork of renowned artist Linda Lee, who captures Carolyn's words with her drawings. And if that wasn't enough, each section includes a link to heavenly inspired music by renowned artist, composer and arranger, Jon Day that brings the stories alive in unexpected ways. And each section is then followed with a thought-provoking devotional written by counselor, public speaker, and teacher, Paul Day, PhD! This wonderful book is designed for those who want more than the superficial. **"A View From Heaven"** will awaken the senses of your heart to the much more revelation of the Father! Happy reading!

Brian and Candice Simmons, The Passion Translation

Often, we will pray and see the results of the prayer but never realize the magnificent involvement of the heavenly realm. Carolyn Neary is a gifted seer, intercessor and prophetic voice for the Church. In her new book, *A View From Heaven*, you will see the majestic ensemble of heaven revealed in beautiful yet simple to understand concepts. As Carolyn describes her encounters with the Lord and His angelic hosts, she brings understanding and practical steps in working with the angelic. The descriptions of these encounters and the practical devotional that follows by Dr. Paul Day will bring a fullness of life to your relationship with the Lord and help you realize the power of your prayers. When you read this book you will be drawn into a deeper encounter with the Lord.

Paul Martini, Global Awakening Evangelist

The book **A View From Heaven** is creative and unique is so many ways. Carolyn Neary, Linda Lee, Jon Day and Dr. Paul Day have done a wonderful job of using their gifts to point people to Jesus through this book. I personally love the picture with the story titled Alabaster Jar and its activations. I am proud of this team for following their hearts and passions. May all who read this book be inspired to fall more in love with Jesus.

Chris Overstreet, Evangelism and Discipleship Pastor. Bethel Church

I'm so excited to recommend this new book by my friend, Carolyn Neary. She has been a key intercessor for my family and me for a while. Some people work for God, some know about God and then there are those who develop a friendship with God. I know her to be a friend of God. Jesus told us that He delights in sharing His secrets with His friends. This book contains the rewards of a prophet, seer and friend of God who has diligently sought the Lord in the secret place. This book has been in the Library of Heaven for a while and is now being made available to you and me. Enjoy.

Richie Seltzer, Imagine Church, Lead Pastor, Evangelist

If you are looking to grow to a deeper and more intimate place of spirituality, this book is going to inspire you to that and more. Carolyn and Paul are two of the most sincere people I know and have inspired many people to have incredible Kingdom encounters. The collaboration of talent gathered in this book will touch your senses and your heart as you meditate upon the words, images and truths. This would be such a great book to go through as a couple or small group.

Jennifer Taylor, Author

I have the privilege of knowing Carolyn as my very dear friend and a friend of God who always desires to walk with a pure heart towards Him. "Blessed are the pure in heart for they shall see God". In this must-read book **A View from Heaven**, Carolyn, Paul, Linda and Jon have captured a glimpse of the richness of the heavenlies that will inspire and challenge each of its readers to have a deeper and a powerful experience of walking with God daily.

Anita Augustine, Family Physician, Living Hope Centre

A View From Heaven is truly a unique reading experience. It is filled with rich descriptive pictures that will fill the readers' spiritual senses with wonder. Carolyn Neary's heavenly experiences are both amazing and very revealing of heavenly matters. The devotional sections by Dr. Paul Day are designed to help the reader get the maximum benefit from Carolyn's heavenly encounters. You will also love the very beautiful illustrations by Linda Lee and music scores by Jon Day. I highly recommend this book to all who want to know more about Heaven and the heart of our Heavenly Father.

Ben Peters, Speaker, Author, Co-Founder of Kingdom Sending Centre

Acknowledgements

I lovingly dedicate this book to my dear sister, Rosemary Jean.
"You will seek me and find me when you seek me with all your heart."
Jeremiah 29:13 (NIV)

There are so many I would like to acknowledge and thank for bringing **A View From Heaven** to life.

To Dr. Paul Day (devotionals), Linda Lee (artwork) and Jon Day (music), I sincerely thank each of you for offering your giftedness to this project to bring these visions to life in ways beyond what I could ever have imagined.

To the "Team" – Bill Neary, Paul and Linda Day, Craig and Jennifer Taylor and Jon Day thanks for your unwavering support and counsel on the journey to getting this project to publication.

To Brian and Candice Simmons, and all the endorsers, thank you for your encouragement and kind words of support for this project.

To Barry and Nadine Pawlak – thanks for helping to get this project of the ground.

To Dr. Paul Day, thank you for your continual encouragement, wisdom, organizing and editing of the manuscript, seeing and believing in the value and potential of this project.

To Amanda Taylor, for your masterful editing.

To the team at Westbow Press, thank you for believing in this project and helping us share it with the masses.

To Susan Ruzek, for putting your money where your heart is.

To the many friends who have prayed for and encouraged me to produce **A View From Heaven.**

To my dear husband, Bill Neary and my family, especially my precious grandchildren – Aria, Poet, William, and Victoria – I always look forward to any opportunity to tell the world how much I love all of you.

Contents

Backstory ix
Introduction xi

Prayer
    Art 2
    Vision 3
    Devotional 5

Angels
    Art 8
    Vision 9
    Devotional 12

Alabaster Jar
    Art 16
    Vision 17
    Devotional 19

Owl
    Art 24
    Vision 25
    Devotional 27

Desert
    Art 30
    Vision 31
    Devotional 34

The Jewellery Box
    Art 38
    Vision 39
    Devotional 41

Keys
    Art 46
    Vision 47
    Devotional 49

Pentecost
    Art 52
    Vision 53
    Devotional 58

Backstory

As long as I (Carolyn) can remember, I have seen, felt and heard things from the supernatural world. It has taken me many years to realize that this is both a gift and a blessing from God.

I did not grow up in a church-going home. My home fostered unconditional love and my parents provided an environment where we were able to experience many areas of interest such as sports, education, and travel. However, talking about God was limited and things of the supernatural world were all but non-existent in our family. Nevertheless, feeling the presence of a supernatural world was as normal for me as feeling the natural world.

When I was sixteen, I spent the summer months as a lifeguard at a Bible camp a few hours from the little town in which I grew up. As one of the staff, I had my own cabin. One night, lying in my bunk, I decided it was time to be serious about talking to God to see if He was real. After all, I was at a Bible camp!

In the quiet of my tiny cabin, I said out loud, "Jesus, if You are real, show me and I will serve You with my whole heart." Instantly, the cabin filled with light and a feeling of peace washed over me. I felt a gentle breeze enter my room and it brushed against my skin. I was neither scared nor shocked as I had sensed this Presence before. That night, I accepted Jesus as my Saviour. It was a wonderful night of angelic visits. It was also the start of experiencing many heavenly visions and visitations, some of which I want to share with you in this book.

Here's the backstory to each of those encounters (in the order they appear in the book).

Since I was a child, I've been intrigued by the thought that everything we do creates a reaction. As a person of prayer, I've always carried a conviction that when we pray, in whatever form, much like the butterfly effect, we cause a huge reaction in heaven. Years ago, while lying in bed during the wee hours of the morning, I was mesmerized by one of the very first visions I experienced. I watched myself climb a hill. As I reached its peak, it took my breath away witnessing the realities of prayer and what it looks like from the view of heaven. I described what I saw in the story titled **Prayer**.

Years later, I attended a worship service at a little country church with my son-in-law. As we arrived where the service was being held, I saw a massive army of angels all around the entire property. The angels were comprised of many different shapes and sizes. Somehow, without conversation, I knew that they all had different purposes and held different weapons. Some were walking the property, some sitting on the roof of the building, and all were very alert to the activity of the evening. I outlined what I saw in the story titled **Angels**.

One afternoon, a few months ago, while meditating in quiet, I saw a vision of a jar. I recognized it as an alabaster jar filled with a liquid that was gold in colour. The liquid moved like it had life in it. I asked the Lord what it meant. He impressed on my heart that the golden substance represented His Spirit. It was expanding, overflowing, and touching the world. Then I saw the jar in the hands of a young woman. As I watched her, I smelled a mixture of cinnamon, myrrh, frankincense, and the sweetness of Jasmine and Lily of the Valley. I could sense her emotional pain. Then I saw her journey from pain and shame to hope and freedom. I wrote about this vision in the story titled **Alabaster Jar**.

Days before travelling to a renowned city in Alberta to lead a group of spiritual leaders in a prayer walk, I descended a hill on my favorite country walk and heard the haunting call of a majestic Barn Owl. When I turned to watch the great bird, I looked into a crevasse of the earth which activated a vision and hearing things that the earth has been holding for generations. I have written about that encounter in the story titled **Owl.**

A little more than a year ago, I was feeling a great burden to pray for some dear people whom I love. As I entered into my prayer closet, the comfort of my room disappeared into a vision of a fiery desert. I felt the anguish of the people for whom I was praying. That burden transformed into a vision I have written about titled **Desert.**

Not long ago, I started to see what appeared to be sparkles in my peripheral vision. Over the next couple days, the sparkles continued turning into flashing lights, and finally, explosive lights. I asked the Lord what this was. I heard in my heart the word "gems." I began searching the scriptures and Internet to learn more about gems. I was amazed to discover many Biblical references to gems and jewels that I had never heard of. I also found several articles and videos about gems and gold dust appearing in worship services. I asked the Lord to explain these things. I heard that He has woven the beauty of heaven right into our DNA. We are not broken mistakes, but His priceless treasures. I wrote about this vision and encounter in the story titled **Jewelry Box**.

While speaking at a camp last year, I witnessed an unusual amount of angelic activity. One evening, I was sitting in a worship practice soaking up the beautifully sung words from the worship leader when all of a sudden I saw the roof of the building being torn away. I was left viewing the open nighttime sky! The stars were so bright, it seemed I might be able to reach out and touch them. I saw the angelic hosts. I heard the voice of the Lord in my heart say that even the stars memorize the songs we sing about Him. In the service that followed, several of us witnessed an angel wrap its wings around one young woman who needed a little extra comfort. We were amazed as we witnessed her settle right before our eyes. I have written about this experience in the story titled **Keys**.

During the last Pentecost season, I asked the Lord if I could see and feel what those present on the Day of Pentecost experienced (Acts 2:1-41). Immediately, I felt myself enter into days long ago and began to see and feel many things. I was so overwhelmed by the experience that I was unable to articulate it clearly until after meeting with Dr. Paul Day. He helped me recognize and clarify the vision I saw. It blows my mind that the Lord allowed me to see a view from the eyes of a young, first century girl watching and holding these stories. The story is titled **Pentecost**

The stories that I have written are visitations that I had from our Heavenly Father. I'm sharing them to encourage the body of Christ that the supernatural world is as real as the natural world. I'm convinced God has opened the door for everyone to see, feel and perceive beyond the natural world. I have met so many people that see and feel in the supernatural world in varied and unique ways. I want to encourage you to seek for more. One thing that I know for sure – when we seek Him, we will surely find Him.

Carolyn Neary

Introduction

"You will find Me, when you seek Me with all your heart." (Jeremiah 29:13 NIV)

This is a remarkable promise with profound possibilities. And it's a promise that is found throughout the scriptures.

As progeny of the Enlightenment, so often we tend to place our focus on the part of this promise that we can do and measure – the science of "seeking", while holding only a fragile and tentative belief that our Heavenly Father will actually honor His part of the promise and allow us to find Him.

How many have been frustrated and disappointed, even to the point of giving up, because they employed prescribed methods of seeking without any finding? How many have put their faith in recommended prayer or Bible study strategies in hopes they would experience something, anything? But instead, experienced silence?

Pondering this dilemma left me (Paul) wondering if the blockage so many experience is not a matter of strategy, but doubt – doubt about whether the Father will actually open their ears to hear His voice. Have we, as spiritual leaders and mentors, mistakenly led others to believe it's their personal responsibility to crack the "hearing code" when, in fact, only He can open their ears?

For a moment, let's consider one of Peter's more spectacular encounters with Jesus.

Matthew 14:22-33 details an impossible meeting between Jesus and Peter, on the surface of the sea. Jesus didn't invite Peter based on Peter's sophisticated theological understanding or knowledge of a hidden loophole in the natural law of gravity or water density. The truth is, nothing Peter knew or did could make the water hold him. It was Jesus' authority over the water that facilitated their meeting on the surface of the water.

What Peter was able to do was choose to accept Jesus' invitation and step beyond the boundaries of what he knew and understood about the properties of water, beyond the safety of the boat's proven buoyancy, and beyond the boundary of his faith to encounter the One with authority over heaven and earth in an impossible meeting place.

The same is true of the invitation in Jeremiah 29:13. It's not about uncovering some hidden hearing code or mantra that will open our spiritual eyes and ears. It's about what He can do, what He is waiting to do, wanting to do – so we encounter Him in what seems an impossible meeting place.

Sadly, many conclude it is best to lower expectations about actually encountering Him and adopt a theological position they consider "more reasonable." But by doing so, they unwittingly convert the Father's wide open invitation to an adventure of intimacy into a focus and discipline of various forms of prayer and Bible study as an end in itself.

Please hear me clearly. I'm not challenging the importance of prayer and Bible study. They are the lifelines of the spiritual life. But, I do want to expose the vulnerability of limiting our faith about "finding" in response to frustration or disappointment. While it might feel safer to settle for understanding over encounter, doing so risks forfeiting one of the greatest gifts and benefits of our spiritual adoption – intimacy with Our Father.

So, what if we approached Jeremiah 29:13 as an invitation rather than a task? What if we read the text with an emphasis on Our Father's ability to be found rather than our ability to seek?

He wants to be found. He wants to be known. He has been waiting for you to arrive at this moment in history to make Himself known to you. Imagine waiting, since before the foundations of the world, to reveal to your children who you really are.

Jesus never promises something He hasn't already seen. He didn't invite Peter out of the boat hoping the water would hold him. He knew it would. He had already seen it happen. In the same way, Jeremiah 29:13 isn't offered to us as a hopeful possibility, but a reality waiting to be experienced. He has already witnessed you hearing His voice.

Through the prophet Joel (2:28), our Sovereign Lord declared "I will" pour out My Spirit on all people, and "they will" prophesy, dream dreams, see visions. He wills, so we can. He pours out prophesies, dreams, and visions for us to receive. He has already determined specific prophesies, dreams, and visions for you. He has already seen you receiving and sharing them.

Would you be willing to expand the boundary of your faith and trust Him to open your spiritual eyes and ears? If so, would you be willing to declare, by faith, "I hear the voice of the Shepherd because He has opened my spiritual ears to hear His voice" and "I see kingdom visions and dreams because He has opened my spiritual eyes to see what He is doing and what He wants to do with and through me?"

This book is not about ways to seek after Him. It's a book about what can happen when we find Him. He rewards those who diligently seek Him (Hebrews 11:6). This book is a collection of rewards and evidences of finding Him that include visions and dreams. When we seek Him, we not only find Him, but He begins to reveal more and more of the mysteries of the unseen realm.

This book has been written to inspire you to believe wholeheartedly that He will help you find Him, the Revealer of Mysteries (Daniel 2:29).

When Jesus appeared to His disciples in the midst of the Sea of Galilee, eleven remained in the boat. Only one dared to challenge the boundaries of his faith and join Jesus in an impossible meeting place. We hope this book inspires you to be one who will dare to do the same.

This book is the result of a unique collaboration. The project started out as a simple collection of visions and dreams seen and experienced by Carolyn Neary, some on prayer walks, some during the night, some during ministry times. Having prayed about what she was to do with these revelations, Carolyn felt led to invite renowned artist, Linda Lee to collaborate with art pieces that captured the heart of these visitations. After further prayer, Carolyn felt led to invite me to write devotionals motivated by each vision to inspire you, the reader, to seek to "see and hear" more. A few months later, Carolyn and I felt led to ask my younger brother, Jon to compose the equivalent of a movie score for each story. What he composed and orchestrated will take your experience to a whole new level. Together, we invite you to a multi-sensory journey.

Each chapter includes art, story, music and devotional reflection. We encourage you to take a moment to reflect on Linda's inspired artwork before reading the story of Carolyn's vision. After reading through the story once, we encourage you to read it a second time while listening to the music sound track (available at www.jdaymusic.com) that Jon was inspired to create to bring the story to life. Then, when you're ready, take some time to read through the devotional and reflection questions with expectation of a heavenly encounter.

Dr. Paul Day

Project Team

Carolyn Neary is a captivating speaker, inspired minister, and a vibrant mother and grandmother. As a newlywed and young mom, Carolyn devoted her earlier years to intercession and quietly developing a deep, rich relationship with her Maker. Over that time, her career path developed from wide-ranging positions like medic and flight attendant. She began emerging as a speaker and minister in her children's teen years, developing and leading prayer teams at international events, and ministering to leaders in the business world.

In 2013, Carolyn was inspired to write a children's book "*Gifts From Grandma's Garden*," encouraging all ages to be generous and thoughtful. An anti-bullying tale, "*Always Room For One More*," featuring delightful and unforgettable forest creatures, followed in 2015. Now, with "*A View From Heaven*," Carolyn aims to inspire adults to see themselves and the spiritual world around them a little differently.

Carolyn lives in Calgary, Canada, with her husband Bill (m. 78'). To book Carolyn to speak at an event, please contact her at Nearycarolyn@gmail.com.

Dr. Paul Day has devoted his life to fulfilling the Isaiah 61:1-3 calling he received as a teenager. After twenty years of full-time church ministry and operating a part-time counseling practice in various cities in Canada and the U.S., Paul relocated his family to Panama in 2007, where he served as director of a humanitarian initiative for five years. Upon his return to Canada in 2012, he restarted his counselling practice full-time. In early 2013, Paul had a "burning bush" encounter that opened up a greater awareness and understanding of the spirit realm and the spiritual freedom process which shifted his life and ministry focus.

Paul is a sought-after public speaker, teacher, and trainer focusing on trauma recovery, spiritual freedom, spiritual warfare, and intimacy with the Father. He completed a M.A. in Theology and a PhD in Marriage and Family Therapy at Fuller Theological Seminary (Pasadena, CA).

He and his wife, Linda (m. 90') and their two teenage kids live in Calgary, Canada. To contact Paul to speak at an event, please contact him at drpaulday@gmail.com. For more info: *www.drpaulday.com*

Linda Lee began experimenting with graphic design in 1996, as she worked with her pastor and friend, Bill Johnson, learning to create art for the covers of his teaching series. She eventually started exploring "photo montage" and found that this type of art allowed her to express, in great detail, different spiritual experiences she had been having with God. In 2007, she began selling prints of her art and has had the pleasure of hearing testimonies from around the world of how God uses it to draw people into His presence. It is to this end that Linda continues to create. "*My desire is to create visual experiences of heavenly encounters and to stir hunger in the hearts of people to pursue and encounter the love of God for themselves,*" she says, quoting, "*Taste and see that the Lord is good*" (Psalms 34:8 NIV).

Linda has been working for Bethel Church in Redding, CA as a graphic designer since 1996. She also served for many years as a worship leader, including leading the worship ministry for her home church in Weaverville, CA before relocating to Redding in 2009.

She and her husband Steve (m. 78') are currently residing in Redding, CA where they enjoy being close to two of their three children and their six grandchildren. For more info: *www.lindaleecreates.com* or *www.lindaleecreates.myshopify.com*

Jon Day is a sought after performer, composer, orchestrator, director, and educator of music. Several of his compositions and orchestrations have been featured on award-winning and nominated albums in Canada. Jon spent more than a decade in church music and arts ministry in both Canada and the U.S.

After several years traveling and working abroad, Jon returned with his family to Calgary, Canada in 2013 to begin teaching university music and theatre arts. A few years later, Jon had a powerful encounter with God that changed his perception and awareness of the spirit realm, and sent him on a new path of musical creativity.

For more info, to listen to the music scores for ***A View From Heaven*** or to contact Jon: www.jdaymusic.com

PRAYER

Link to music score:
www.jdaymusic.com

The Hill

The walk up the hillside was beautiful, easier than I thought, and surprisingly quick. I'm not sure why I waited so long to pursue the summit. It seemed like minimal time and effort to comfortably stroll to the top. There was even a perfect tree to lean against to view the panoramic sights below.

The Sound

I was nudged from a peaceful daydream by the sound of singing and music. It was a sound that I had never heard before, perhaps of a language that had not yet been vocalized. It rang across the valley in harmonies that were precise and pure, in tones no human could be capable of. Yet its words were sweet, and somehow I understood them.

The sound of singing was loud and quiet, close and far. I felt as if it had weight and flavour. I could feel it rest in my hands and taste it on the edges of my lips.

I wanted to sing along as it seemed a familiar tune. I was not sure if I had just witnessed the birth of a new aria. My senses were alive and excited, but also at peace and rest.

The Lights

I was about to open my mouth to sing along when lights vaulted across the sky. They were magnificent, dancing from the North to the South, then weaving and exploding from West to East. The magnitude of the size and colors of the lights exhausted my vocabulary of description. They continued to rise from some unknown origin faster than my eyes could follow. They revealed colours and designs that were more graphic than a child's imagination. They lit up an already clear and bright sky.

The Smells

I was going to stand to applaud the array of dancing beams when I became nearly intoxicated with fragrances assaulting my senses. It smelled like a memory of home, peace, and love entwined. Where did the aroma of fragrances originate – my mother's womb, a compilation of years of Christmas trees, nearly forgotten hopes and dreams?

The Secrets

The fragrances mixed with memories and began to leak from my eyes. That is when I could barely contain the weight of pleasure. I felt the heaviness of a hand pushing on my chest. I could tell that secret treasures, things not meant to be exposed, were being pulled from my insides. It was wonderfully scary and like a death that brought life.

Years of pain and stiffness left my body, youth made my bones journey with the Eagle and laughter filled my lungs. Some hidden joy that was full of nonsense wiggled its way from my toes to my mouth, pushing back years of gravel and bumps. Velvet strips of peace brushed over my skin and there was no question that something spectacular had willingly visited me.

This all took place in a moment, in a lifetime.

With both a lightness in my heart and a longing in my soul, I started down the path to the bottom of the hill. I didn't want to leave, but I was drawn to the bottom to seek answers to my experience.

The Sage

As I slowly followed the worn path toward the bottom of the hill, I met an old Sage walking up. He asked if I had reached the top.

I told him of my experience and how I longed for the pictures I saw to flash through my eyes, ears, and heart again.

He graciously quenched my need for understanding by explaining that what I had seen were sights from Heaven's view. Before I could ask, "What could possibly cause these sights to happen?" the Sage rested his aged, old hand on his heart and began to explain that each song I heard in the breeze, every light I saw in my heart, all the aromas of blessing I smelled, were caused by one thing.

I begged him to tell me.

He smiled as a gentle tear slid from his eyes. He beckoned me to draw closer.

He told me I was watching prayer.

PRAYER DEVOTIONAL

"Another angel, who had a golden censer, came and stood at the altar. He was given much incense to offer, with the prayers of all God's people, on the golden altar in front of the throne. The smoke of the incense, together with the prayers of God's people, went up before God from the angel's hand." (Revelation 8:3-4 NIV)

What a scene!

Before our Father's throne rises an unrelenting stream of our petitions, intercessions, worship, and declarations. Our prayers are remembered, never forgotten, each expression an act of trust that ministers to His heart.

We tend to think of "ministry" in terms of "heaven to earth" (He ministers to us), not so much "earth to heaven" (we minister to Him). It's true that He doesn't relate to us out of need. But offering Him our pain, tears, and questions is a trust-response that ministers to His heart.

It touches His heart when we trust Him enough to bring the intimate matters of our heart and mind to Him. It's evidence of the effectiveness of His Holy Spirit to draw us into a life-giving exchange – our ashes for His crown of beauty, our mourning for His joy, our garment of despair for His garment of gladness (Isaiah 61:1-3).

Can you imagine the colors, sounds, tastes, smells, and sensations He experiences in transacting Isaiah 61 exchanges?

Carolyn's vision of prayer as song, dancing colors, and a pleasing fragrance unveils how much there is for us to experience and know about the spiritual realities of prayer.

As human beings, we have many senses. There are the five primary senses: sight, sound, smell, taste, and touch. But there are other finer senses like pressure, itch, hot and cold, tension, pain, balance, direction, thirst, hunger, magnetic pull, and time, to name a few.

There are some unique individuals who experience a blending of multiple senses. But for most of us, we don't feel colors or hear an aroma. We generally experience our senses separately.

But He hears color, sees smells, and tastes sounds. Our prayers are not only sounds before Him, but incense smoke that rises before Him, possessing a fragrance that pleases Him.

Imagine, for a minute, if your spiritual eyes were opened to "see" and your spiritual ears to "hear" as He does? What if you could see the color of words, or hear the earth crying out for its liberation (Romans 8:19-21)?

I wonder how an expression of love to our spouse or children tastes to Him or what music He hears accompanying an act of kindness. Or what our words of criticism smell like to Him. Or what He sees as the color of our self-condemning thoughts. Or the temperature of words of mercy and forgiveness that He feels.

I wonder if we might be slower to judge or condemn others if we saw the color and smelled the fragrance of our words as they were about to roll off our lips. What if we could see the color and odour of a declaration of fear? I wonder if it would motivate us to defiantly declare, even in a precarious situation, "I will not be afraid because He is with me." I wonder how it ministers to His heart to witness us making such courageous declarations in the face of fear.

Paul prayed for the Ephesians (1:18) that the Father would "open the eyes of their heart" so they could know the hope to which they were called. I ask the Father to "open your spiritual senses" to discern the colors, sounds, fragrances, flavours, and sensations of your thoughts, words, and actions and those of others.

Practical Application

Take some quiet time, ask Holy Spirit to awaken your spiritual senses and reflect on these questions.

1. What's the fragrance of the meditations of your heart (Psalm 19:14)?
2. What's the color of the words you've recently spoken over your spouse, kids, siblings, parents, and friends (Psalm 19:14)?
3. When you enter a room, what flavour fills the mouths of those with you in the room (2 Corinthians 2:15-16)?
4. What's the temperature of the key relationships in your life (Revelations 3:16)?
5. Have you spoken heavy words over another that Holy Spirit is asking you to lift off and exchange for words of life and blessing (Matthew 5:24, Proverbs 18:21)?
6. What words has the Father spoken over you that are burning inside you (Jeremiah 20:9)?

ANGELS

Link to music score:
www.jdaymusic.com

Creator

I create infinitely. I design from the fabric of space and time. I weave together beings of perfection, lightly dusted with endless possibilities.

Gabriel

I designed Gabriel after the monumental strength of the mountain range that spreads its mightiness of immovability across the horizon. He has the strength of boulders, those foundations for peaks and valleys.

Gabriel has the courage of a mother bear that has seen danger licking its lips, sighting her cubs. He has the persistence and creativity of the waterways that forge new paths around the fiords and muskeg.

Gabriel is My companion, My guard, and My messenger. There are no secrets held between us, but there is no expectation for his Creator to share them. He is an angel of great standing in the community of Heaven.

Warrior Angels

My warrior angels are creations I cannot do without. They gather their forces in endless bravery as they descend to the relative darkness of Earth. They rejoice in sacrificing their own comfort for the possibility of fighting one more battle for My children. They understand the language of war and they speak it fluently.

Their eyes are coloured with the power of My insight as they watch the movements of the spiritual beings crowded around My created Earth. They hover around the warm light of prayer and attack the darkness on instant command.

I rejoice in My army of warrior angels. I say their names with great pride. They are powerful, tireless, and cannot be counted by human numerals. The vastness of the troops that I have sent provides endless victory shrouded in humility. No opposing army can outnumber My resources.

Mercy Angels

My angels of mercy minister to My heart every day. They direct earthbound songs of sorrow until they are heaven-reaching exultations of joy. These angels warmly breathe over cold, dead ashes to resurrect the power of hope and swirl it to envelop My children. They have an endless storehouse of hope, lavishly delivered in personalized robes that uplift and give life. The tempo of their tireless work is fashioned after the ocean's waves that relentlessly splash upon the waiting sand. To pause in their restorative pursuits never occurs to them. Rather, they delight in their task, always applying mercy and hope.

Messenger Angels

Messenger angels delight to carry the golden chest of My words. They follow the current of My will and deliver My words with perfect timing and accuracy. They are never late, but they are always attentive with every opportunity to release the living words of heaven. The messages they utter direct the broken-hearted to the source of wholeness. They speak truth and revelation to the darkest periods of one's history. The words they deliver are washed with the blood of the Risen King, Creator, and Carer of all. Their messages are alive and growing, never stagnant or foul. Each utterance has its own twist and turn, characterizing the uniqueness of its wealth. The communication is delivered in a package that reduces fear. My timing is the seal around the message, a guarantee of perfection. Messenger angels are the delight of My creation. Even heaven rejoices at their sight as they proclaim My heart. I am always for My children – not against – and My messages are impregnated with My perfect love.

Healing Angels

Healing angels are the littlest of the cherubs in heaven. They exhibit the wonder of youth and age end. They sprinkle My healing touch upon the Earth. They make their presence known in ways as varied as droplets in a desert, blooms in a garden, and a flickering fire in a cold wilderness.

They move and flow as molten glass follows the rod in the master's fire. I have gathered the nectar from all of creation and poured it over them. They touch, kiss, and knead their way into the bodies of My Kingdom-builders, My precious children. My healing angels have the most demands. They linger as close as My fingertips, keen for the chance to be sent out to restore. "Let all the children come to me" is their aria. Many bowls of prayer are filled with the need for healing. A secret wealth of physical restoration is perfectly administered by the simple wisp of their wings. The welfare of great kingdoms and their leaders unwittingly balance upon the visitation of these angelic hosts.

Tear Collector Angels

The dearest angels of all, the most precious of My heavenly hosts, have the greatest design. I have tenderly wrapped together the shape of a lamb, the beauty of the butterfly, and the love of a mother's heart and woven all into the fabric of these angels. With the precision of a skilled surgeon, they gently rest on the chest of the broken-hearted, pinpoint a wound and sweetly exchange pain for comfort. These mighty ones are the tear collectors.

They carry their vials made of perfectly cut diamond. The vial is trimmed with jewels that glitter at the sound of My heartbeat. These angels leave their spot in heaven to collect every tear that has been shed. The hands of these angels are tender and pure, never used in battle, never stained with blood, and caressed by the perfect wool of the Lamb.

Tear collectors have a purity that is only revealed at the end of the earthly life. The hands of the collectors understand the treasure they touch. They understand that I hold each tear, each vial to My chest and feel the pain, the joy, the end of dreams, the birth of the new. The tears of My children mingle with Mine and spread into the seas. Every tear has a story. They cascade down the mighty waterfalls and flow to the hidden springs in the deserts. The tear collectors travel only once to Earth; the treasure they carry to Me is so priceless that they exhaust their existence to collect the tears. They are created for one trip. They regard their journey the greatest joy in all creation. My tear collectors hold My heartbeat in their hands.

Heavenly Hosts

Swirling, dancing, raging, ministering, revealing. All of My angels minister My strength, heart, wisdom, and kindness. Each is uniquely created from My heart of boundless love and mercy. Never alone, always surrounded, ready to fight, tolling bells of mercy. At the command of My will, they are created with victory as their shadow.

ANGELS DEVOTIONAL

"The Lord has established His throne in heaven, and His kingdom rules over all. Praise the Lord, you His angels, you mighty ones who do His bidding, who obey His word. Praise the Lord, all His heavenly hosts, you His servants who do His will. Praise the Lord, all His works everywhere in His dominion. Praise the Lord, my soul." (Psalm 103:19-22 NIV)

Angels are, without a doubt, one of the Father's most precious and calculated creations. They have been charged with the most honourable of assignments, fulfilling the declarations pronounced from the Throne.

Can you imagine living with such clarity of identity, purpose and function; to ensure the words of the Father *"will not return empty"* (Isaiah 55:11 NIV)?

Yet, as remarkable and strong as they are (2 Peter 2:10-12, Jude 1:8-10), angels are but fellow servants with us (Revelations 10:10, 22:9). Sadly, so many individuals have abandoned belief in angels, surrendering them to the jurisdiction of the obscure or occult. As a result, many angels remain waiting for us to believe and join them in fulfilling the Father's will to bring His kingdom *"on earth as it is in heaven"* (Matthew 6:10 NIV).

There's so much to be said about angels. But let's consider a few basic truths.

First, angels relate to us based on who the Father says we are. They see us as the Father sees us. Their first and lasting impression of us is from Him. This means, if we stumble and fall, they don't hold their own judgment over us. They operate in seamless agreement with the One and Only True Judge. They know we are His inheritance and that they have been sent to strengthen and lead us out of our struggles and into our kingdom position as sons and daughters and into our kingdom destiny.

Second, angels know the realities and dynamics of the spirit realms. They know Who rules over the heavens, the earth, and all creation. They know the scope of the authority and power of the Father, Son, and Holy Spirit. Angels know the power of the kingdom of darkness. But as veterans of the conflict, they possess intimate knowledge of the limits and strategies of their foes. Angels know our stories. They've studied us. They know our tendencies and vulnerabilities. Angels have heard the Father's declaration of our kingdom identity, purpose, and assignment and they know their role in ensuring His purposes for us (Job 42:2, Romans 8:28, Philippians 2:13).

Third, angels are constantly involved in our lives. Consider these two stories as told by the gospel writer, Luke.

In his gospel (22:39-46), Luke describes how Jesus suffered great anguish and testing in the garden on the Mount of Olives, just hours before His arrest. Luke noted, as His suffering reached a crescendo, Jesus' declared, *"Father, if You are willing, take this cup from Me; yet not My will, but Yours be done"* (Luke 22:42 NIV), and immediately an angel was sent to strengthen and enable Him to pray more earnestly.

Have you ever faced a time of testing beyond what you thought you were able to bear, asked for strength and then experienced a measure of comfort and a strength, not your own, that got you through the testing?

In Acts 12:1-17, Luke records the miraculous story of Peter being startled from his sleep by an angel who broke off his prison shackles and told him to put on his coat and follow him out of his prison cell. Having reached a point beyond the prison gates, the angel left, and Peter made his way to the home of John's mother where believers had gathered to pray for his release. Luke records that Peter's knock on the door was met with a shocked young woman who ran to tell those gathered that Peter was at the door. Their response is so telling of the spiritual norm of the day. They said, *"You must be out of your mind...It must be his angel"* (Acts 12:15 NIV).

Can you imagine anyone responding like that today? It begs the question, what's happened to our belief and awareness of the presence and function of angels?

So often, discussions of the spiritual realm are anchored in Paul's vivid description of spiritual darkness captured in his letter to the Ephesians, *"For our struggle is not against flesh and blood, but against the rulers, against the authorities, against the powers of this dark world and against the spiritual forces of evil in the heavenly realms"* (Ephesians 6:12 NIV).

But it's imperative that we keep in mind, Jesus is the Head over every ruler and authority (Colossians 2:10) and angels in His Kingdom are more in number and operate with an authority mightier than those of the kingdom of darkness (2 Kings 6:8-17).

So when you are in a spiritual battle, know that experienced warrior angels have been assigned to contend on your behalf to realize the victory Jesus has already secured on the cross. When you ask for help, be it for strength or healing or comfort, know that the Father hears and releases a seasoned ministering angel to carry out His response to your prayer. When you hear a prompting from Holy Spirit to say or do something, know that you have already been assigned the necessary angelic support to help you fulfil His prompting.

Practical Application

1. If you've held guardedness or skepticism in your heart and mind, or even dismissed the reality of angels, would you be willing to open your heart and mind to learn more about your "fellow servants?"
2. Access a Bible app (e.g. Bible Gateway) that offers word searches, type "angel" in the search field, and take some time to read about any of the hundreds of references to angels and how they fulfilled His words (Psalm 103:20).
3. Take time to thank the Father for the angels He has assigned to you.
4. Start each day welcoming the angels He has assigned to you.
5. Take time, at the start of your day, to ask the Father what He would like you, and the angels He has assigned to you, to accomplish.

ALABASTER JAR

Link to music score:
www.jdaymusic.com

Broken Pieces

My daily existence had unravelled into a treadmill of pain, failure, and lost hope. I felt broken into a collection of countless, splintered pieces, including fragments of remains from my bloodline – their vows and actions added streaks of tar, black and heavy.

New Song

But today, I awakened to see a song that filled the atmosphere, each note glistening on the particles of air. I quickly breathed in, inhaling the atoms into my parched and empty lungs. I had never experienced such a thing. I didn't hear it with my natural ears. I didn't see it with my natural sight. I perceived it in my heart.

Alabaster Jar

I reached for the most precious item I owned, my alabaster jar. It was sturdy and beautifully sculpted from gypsum into a perfectly shaped container that carried the oils of release from my fractured heart. The perfectly dried wax seal ensured the golden substance inside was secure. I kept my jar hidden from view. Few people knew of the treasure inside.

My alabaster jar never judged me. It never told me of the ugliness I felt I exuded. I knew that the contents were purchased by shame, yet its value was priceless. It faithfully reminded me that I have a destiny of greatness.

The Plan

I knew of my plan for only a few hours, yet somehow it felt as though it had been entombed, deep inside me, for my whole life. The night before, I rehearsed my actions over and over until the resolve in my heart was like the foundation of the Mount of Olives, unmoving.

I carried my alabaster jar to the place of meeting with fear but also with joy – an emotion I'd never befriended.

The men would not have let me past the guarded ground if they knew what I was going to do next. I let the song that awoke me calm my pounding heart and capture the focus of my mind's eye. There were so many people, but I slid through the crowd like a vapour. It could only have been the song that hid me.

The Encounter

I released the pins from my hair and knelt to let the strands cascade to the Master's feet. As His eyes met mine, I could no longer hear the scolding of the hissing crowd. I was arrested by His love, the complete embrace of His eyes. I was enveloped in the melody. I could hear redemption, see freedom, feel hope for my future.

The seal on the alabaster jar gave way more easily than I expected, as if its contents couldn't bear to wait any longer to join the song. The fragrance of cinnamon, myrrh, and frankincense exploded into the room and filled me to a state of intoxication. It was a time of perfection.

The Exchange

He knew me. He knew the source of my shame. But with each breath, an exchange transacted; my failures for something that was beyond price – kindness, acceptance, worth and trust. The exchange permanently relieved me of the weight of my life to allow me to start anew. I sensed that bringing my failings to Him was somehow an even sweeter gesture than the costly oil. He seemed honoured by my trust.

He told me He had been waiting for me. For me! I poured the costly oil onto the One whose love for me transcended price. Love unconditional, limitless, gracious, complete. He was worth every last drop.

The crowd, still breathless with horror – or perhaps wonder – was unwittingly bathed in the heavy fragrance that proclaimed the new levity of my life. I and the One I love were the only ones whose skin touched the sweet oil, but everyone left with it in their nostrils, glistening on their hair and dancing on their robes.

New Life

The alabaster jar was emptied of the lifeless shards of regret. Then, as if it had always been in the jar, hidden from my searching heart, my jar was full again. Filled with the fresh fragrance of youth, sweet hope for a future filled with purpose.

Life born again.

ALABASTER JAR DEVOTIONAL

"For when she poured this perfume on My body, she did it to prepare Me for burial. Truly I say to you, wherever this gospel is preached in the whole world, what this woman has done will also be spoken of in memory of her." (Matthew 26:12-13 NIV)

What an interaction!

Although the oil was only poured on Jesus, the fragrance stained everyone present. All breathed in the same bouquet. Everyone's clothes reeked with the same expensive scent. It was in them. It was on them.

Adding intrigue, Jesus made it clear to everyone that He welcomed her gesture as an act of burial preparation. But He hadn't experienced death yet, or even His trial. So why did the Father choose to have His Son prepared for burial in this public display, by this specific woman, in such a crowded and intimate setting?

It got me wondering whether something else might have been going on. This story reminded me of another very public and intimate encounter that Jesus had with a woman while surrounded by a room of accusers.

In the gospel of John (8:1-11), the author narrates a dramatic account of a woman caught in adultery by the Pharisees, who then thrust her into the midst of the crowd listening to Jesus as He taught in the Temple. Adding to her shame, the Pharisees interrupted Jesus with a challenge, *"the Law says to stone her, what do You say?"* With a few choice words, *"You without sin, cast the first stone,"* He dismantled the religious façade that artificially identified the woman as the lone sinner and expanded the identification of the defendant from one to all. At once, the teachers of the law, who had arrived with sanctioned instruments of justice in hand, ready to satisfy the rule of the law, quietly abandoned their place in the Temple – a prophetic manifestation of the unseen work of the cross to remove our accusers. In an interesting twist, the Pharisees had unwittingly become participants in a dramatic act of grace for all to witness and experience.

In a similar way, I wonder if Jesus allowed Himself to be prepared for burial in such a public way on purpose.

Consider this.

What if this burial preparation wasn't only for Him? What if it was also for everyone else present? What if the fragrance each one inhaled was actually preparing them to be buried with Him, so they could also be raised to new life in Him?

*"We were therefore buried with him through baptism into death in order that, just as Christ was raised from the dead through the glory of the Father, we too may live a new life. For if we have been united with him in a death like his, we will certainly also be united with him in a resurrection like his. For we know that our old self was crucified with him so that the body ruled by sin might be done away with, that we should no longer be slaves to sin — because anyone who has died has been set free from sin. Now if we died with Christ, we believe that we will also live with him. For we know that since Christ was raised from the dead, he cannot die again; death no longer has mastery over him. **The death he died, he died to sin once for all; but the life he lives, he lives to God.**" (Romans 6:4-10 NIV)*

I think the alabaster story holds an invitation for us.

Jesus knew what it took for her to acquire the expensive perfume; even that it was used for questionable purposes to secure more of it. But clearly, Jesus didn't mind being identified with her or by the fruits of her labour.

In fact, I think it actually ministered to Him. She seemed to have understood who He really was, and why He really came, and that He was willing to absorb her sins, her death penalty, and burial into His story, and that He truly did have the authority to give her new life. It was a humble and trusting act that honoured His redemptive assignment, something even his closest disciples seemed to struggle to grasp.

As she emptied her alabaster jar, the fragrance reached farther and farther, being inhaled by more and more of those present. And I don't think this was a mistake or waste. I think it was a prophetic act of amazing grace.

Although none of them asked to be prepared for the burial of their "old life", the fragrance graciously united each of them with Him. Though all were prepared for burial, only One needed to give His life.

What a beautiful picture of the gospel of grace.

Practical Application

1. Are you carrying internal remnants of your failures and mistakes, or unwanted souvenirs of the sins of others against you, that need to be poured out and emptied on Him? Maybe guilt, shame, sadness, regret, defilement, disappointment, resentment, anger, fear of the opinions of others. He is waiting for you to pour it on Him so He can fill those places in your heart.
2. Sometimes we struggle to let things go. Here's a prayer exercise that might help you "pour out" and "get refilled."
    a. Go to your kitchen. Get a glass. (The glass represents you, a container).
    b. Go to your kitchen sink and fill up the glass with water. (The water represents all that you are carrying inside).
    c. Acknowledge to Him all the past, present, and future burdens you're carrying (e.g. hurt, fear, worries, shame, unforgiveness, sorrow, etc.).
    d. Would you be willing to trust Him with all that you've been carrying? If so, when you're ready, pour out the water as an act of trust. Pour it out and watch it go down the drain. Let it go and trust He will be at work on your behalf regarding all those concerns.
    e. Now for the exchange. It's never His intent they we live on empty. Fill the glass back up with water.
    f. Ask for what you need. Maybe you need to be filled with more of His love to push out fear, or His comfort to soothe wounded places, or His peace to govern your mind, or His joy to be your strength. Ask Him for whatever you need.
    g. Then, when you're ready, take it and drink it. Receive what He has for you.

Here's two important lessons related to "pouring out" and "refilling."

First, if we choose to carry a full glass of "yesterday's burdens" into today, when we ask for His strength or courage or whatever it is that we need, He is rendered powerless to give it to us. Our glass is already full.

We've made our choice to hold onto those things. He will always first ask, "Would you be willing to trust me with what you're carrying, and let it go?" Once we pour out, then there's room to receive.

Second, when we ask for what we need, what we receive is not meant to last. Now before you get upset, let me explain. Let's take joy as an example. We are meant to have joy all the time and have it be our strength. But today's joy is not meant to last into tomorrow. We get a hint of this truth in the Lord's Prayer, which instructs us to ask for our daily bread. Consider this. He could have designed our natural body to only need to eat once a week, but He designed it to eat multiple times a day. He designed eating to not only be a refuelling process, but a reconnecting process. Hunger keeps us gathering to eat throughout the day. Similarly, He could have designed it so that a dose of His joy lasts for a week, but He designed it that joy runs out so that we keep coming back to Him to get refilled. He wants us to remain close and enjoy all that He has for us. And there's good news – His resources are limitless. This means we can live in a constant supply and never have to go without no matter what our circumstances are.

Link to music score:
www.jdaymusic.com

The Owl's Prowl

The owl's ebony eyes search the land for the slightest movement, flying high in the atmosphere during the time when night and morning clash, where the naked eye cannot see the sparks of darkness and near light collide. The smallest of detail does not escape the expert vision of the mighty hunter. Live creatures and angelic hosts remain in its constant view.

Heaven's Call

The voice of the Great I AM calls to His creation and everything changes.

Continents bend, fracturing the brutality of defilement, drawing the residue of history from its hiding place in the layers of time. The owl witnessed the moving of the nations, the shifting of the land and elements of nature, blending and mixing to birth Heaven's purposes.

The Land's Response

The land calls for redemption. Blood has been poured out in every corner. Pain has been the master of deception, but freedom comes. History calls for the groans of the past to endure the next phase of release.

The owl's eyes spy on the decades past, watching the mingling of dreams and prayers, hopes and expectations revealed as the land reconfigures.

The mountains melt like wax next to the open fire of the Holy Spirit. The pressure of the hand of the Almighty transforms coal into diamonds. The prayers of the Saints are released from their compression into the fresh atmosphere with hope for the new generations.

Redemption Released

The fresh blood of the Son carries freedom into place. The soil is oiled with healing and the cracks release cries of worship. The slaves of torture are set free to rise up for their generation. The hand of the thief is crippled by the shed blood of the Saviour.

Earthquakes resound with the sacred cadence of virtue as the blessings of past generations flow broadly across the permissible ground. Prayers of the saints synchronize with the deposit of the silt of freedom, as the land exhales its covenant with heaven.

Redemption devours the complexity of annual sacrifice. The deposits of intercession screen the obscene. Trauma bonds are released from the ties that have held them in place by the memories of devour. The clusters of tribal secrets are dismissed into volcanic fire, weaving throughout the darkened channels of earth, yearning to explode with unwavering resolve from the birthplace of creation and rain on all inhabitants.

Creation Restored

Intimacy is mandatory in the healing of the land as it announces its urgency for sanctity. Vibrations of worship are mated in an intimate dance with the display of lightning, releasing the power and presence of the Creator. Swirling planets pull and tug on the land to draw pockets of sanctified gold. In the underground caverns, the plates drift seamlessly to their original state at the raw place of purification. Gold, aloes, and pollens are released to anoint the land with the justification of purity. The rebirth of hope comes from the window of reconciliation.

High ground savours the isolated flavours that drip with courage as the ground bursts forth praise.

The records inscribed on the rocks, the stories told to each layer, the treasures deposited in the core, all rise to follow the pearl-coloured feathers of the owl to worship at the footstool of the Great I AM.

OWL DEVOTIONAL

"For all creation waits in eager expectation for the children of God to be revealed. For the creation was subjected to frustration, not by its own choice, but by the will of the One who subjected it, in hope that the creation itself will be liberated from its bondage to decay and brought into the freedom and glory of the children of God. We know that the whole creation has been groaning as in the pains of childbirth right up to the present time." (Romans 8:19-22 NIV)

In the beginning, God created the heavens and the earth, and He saw it was good. And then, our story began.

Have you ever built a new house? Linda and I have designed and built three custom homes. It's such an exciting moment when you finally get the keys and move into an untouched, pristine version of what you imagined. But then, you have to manage an unwelcomed anxiety until someone creates the first nick on a wall or scratch on the untouched hardwood floor. Once perfection gets inhabited, marks, scratches, nicks, dents, spills, and stains are undeniable evidence of our presence.

And so it is with the Earth. It bears the markings and stains of our will, both good and bad. Just as muddy footprints dirty a spotless floor, the Earth has been forced to hold the stains and pain remnants of our actions against one another, other creatures, and the earth itself.

In 1994, a Japanese scientist named Masura Emoto, discovered that water crystals from different sources had different compositions, and that water crystals respond to the influences from their environment, specifically, human thoughts and feelings. He first discovered that water crystals from a tap looked different than water crystals from a river, with each possessing the equivalent of a unique finger print. Even more interesting, he discovered that water crystals bloomed in response to kind words, peaceful music and prayers; and became disfigured when exposed to unkind words, aggressive music, and curses.

This is remarkable and sobering when you consider that roughly 60 per cent of your body is water. This means that every self-condemning thought you've entertained has disfigured water crystals in your body. No wonder our bodies agonize when we feel shame. This also means that when you have raised your voice in frustration or made fun of someone or judged or criticized them, water crystals in their body retract and shrivel. But, it also means that when you believe in, encourage, affirm, inspire or speak words of grace, forgiveness, and life to someone, water crystals in their body expand and reach out in full bloom.

The created order of the spirit-mind-body connection is truly amazing.

And what about creation? Consider this. Seventy per cent of the Earth is covered in water. Topsoil is typically comprised of twenty-five per cent water. Imagine what the Earth is holding – every word spoken and every act recorded upon it.

The author of Genesis vividly describes this dynamic between us and the ground.

*"Now Cain said to his brother Abel, 'Let's go out to the field.' While they were in the field, Cain attacked his brother Abel and killed him. Then the L*ORD *said to Cain, 'Where is your brother Abel?' 'I don't know,' he replied. 'Am I my brother's keeper?' The L*ORD *said, 'What have you done? Listen!*

> ***Your brother's blood cries out to Me from the ground***. *Now you are under a curse and driven from the ground, which opened its mouth to receive your brother's blood from your hand. When you work the ground, it will no longer yield its crops for you. You will be a restless wanderer on the earth.'" (Genesis 4:8-12 NIV)*

The Earth has been a forced witness to the human story – good and bad, blessing and cursing. This got me wondering.

What was it like for the Earth to have Jesus walk upon it, to hear His words, to receive His spilled blood? What is left behind when we walk into a place, full of His Spirit, and speak words of life over others?

Just as we ask Him to cleanse us from our sins, we can also ask Him to cleanse and heal the land where we live, work, and visit. Creation is waiting for us to agree with heaven and begin its liberation from decay.

> *"If my people, who are called by My name, will humble themselves and pray and seek My face and turn from their wicked ways, then I will hear from heaven, and I will forgive their sin and will heal their land." (2 Chronicles 7:14 NIV)*

Practical Application

1. Ask Holy Spirit to cleanse the land where your house is (and any other lands you own) from the remnants of all sins committed on that land – by you and everyone before you. Consecrate the land back to the Father and declare a kingdom blessing over it.
2. Ask Holy Spirit to cleanse your home and to remove the effects of all words and actions that brought pain, division, fear, shame, despair, and heaviness. Consecrate your home back to Him and declare a kingdom blessing over it and everyone who resides with you. Linda and I have consecrated our house as a "House of Peace" ruled by the Prince of Peace (Isaiah 9:6).
3. Take time to "pour out" and "get refilled" (see Alabaster Jar Devotional). Then declare over yourself the Father's blessing, "I am Your son/daughter, I accept that You love me completely as I am, and that I bring You great pleasure" (Matthew 3:17).
4. Let Holy Spirit search the younger places in your heart (Ps 139:23-24). Let Him identify a memory He wants to work on with you. Take back any judgments held in your heart against others in the memory. Ask Holy Spirit to lift off all effects of your judgments upon the other person's body, mind, emotions, and spirit. Declare and release forgiveness and blessing over them. Let Holy Spirit reveal to you the Father's desires for that person and agree with Him in intercession (Romans 8:34).
5. Ask Holy Spirit to cleanse your place of work and declare a kingdom blessing over it, the ownership, the employees, and every customer or client who engages your business. Consider this. The Lord blessed the "household and land" of Potiphar, a general in Pharaoh's army, because Joseph worked for him (Genesis 39:5). In the same way, we can claim blessing for the business and land where we work.
6. Repent on behalf of the sins of your nation and ask Holy Spirit to cleanse the nation where you live. Consecrate your nation's land to the Lord and release His blessing upon it. *"Blessed is the people of whom this is true; blessed is the people whose God is the LORD"* (Psalm 144:15 NIV).

DESERT

Link to music score:
www.jdaymusic.com

Desert Surprise

I'm not sure how it happened. One moment I was young and vibrant, full of dreams and energy. Was it a trick of the mind? Maybe time travel? How could it be that I was middle aged and standing in the midst of the Desert?

At first, I liked the warmth of the sand. But being dressed in business attire, it didn't take long to become uncomfortable. As far as the eye could see, I was surrounded by sand. I decided to sit for a bit, and then it occurred to me that this was real, not a dream. Somehow I knew if I was going to stay alive, I had better not question how I got here. I needed to find shelter.

Letting Go

I started to walk toward some unknown horizon and found that the only way I knew if I was going in a straight line was to look back at my tracks. Bit by bit, I shed my clothes, even the expensive shoes that once showed off my refined taste in elite ware.

Sand that once was welcomed on a long deserved holiday now burrowed its way into every nook of my body. The grit in my mouth pestered my teeth and made me shudder. The sand in my ears muffled the merciless drone of the desert wind. My skin felt as though it was being nipped at by some unseen menace – hot and dry, cracking with every step. I knew I had to find help. I couldn't last much longer.

It was finally time to drop the expensive briefcase that was full of my brilliant ideas. That hurt.

The relentless sun that had been baking my face was slowly slinking behind the horizon, which now seemed impossible to reach. My hopes of rescue became the tyranny of taunts, promises that evaporated like beads of sweat.

Night Time

The darkness encased me like a plastic bag, smothering the flow of oxygen to my lungs. I felt fear pounding in my throat. In the corner of my eyes, I saw the monsters of the Desert flash before me and then disappear, only to assault the secret parts of my mind. Loneliness had climbed upon my shoulders, imposing its pain like the whip of a harsh taskmaster.

The musings about my chosen path had been flitting around the door of my conscious thoughts long before now, a door I had inhospitably slammed shut. Now the frightening questions burst in and demanded attention. How did this happen? How and when did I drop from my world into the middle of this God-forsaken Desert? And how do I get back?

They led me into a paralyzing cloud of the unknown, void of any hope.

Somewhere, somehow, I succumbed to the sweet relief of slumber. But the initial sweetness was no match for my tortured soul. Sleep was not peaceful, not restful, but full of horror – trying to escape the bruising shackles on my mind and emotions.

Another Day

The morning brought it growls of trouble. I survived the night, but how do I go on? Where do I find even a drop of water to quench the metallic taste of death on my tongue? Which direction do I go? Which direction did I come from? All marks of familiarity were gone, erased by the beating of one grain of sand on the other. I was a castaway shouting into the void.

I gently touched my raw fingertip to the corners of my eyes only to be shocked by the deep, stony lines, puffy and weepy, that were etched into my face by the desert elements and, if I'm honest, by the life I'd chosen that brought me here. I could imagine the disfigurement of my appearance.

Another day came and went. I mindlessly took one footstep at a time. How could I quit? It would be sure death. A death all alone, consumed by the monsters of the Desert – regret, weariness, self-recrimination, condemnation, pride, and guilt. The caverns of my heart craved life.

Exodus of Hope

Then, as I observed and considered the sounds and sights of the Desert, I realized I was no longer afraid. Exposing the previously banished questions about my life had somehow muffled the roars of my failures and foolishness. Fear was no longer my devilish companion.

I thought I saw a twinkling of lights on the evasive horizon. Was it a mean childhood trick, reliving the mockery of growing up? Could I dare to embrace the faint flicker of hope I felt buried deep in some corner of my belly? Could the debut of hope usher fear's exit? I stumbled fixedly to the erratic sparks on the horizon.

Now, I traveled with a new confidence, a feeling I thought was lost. A rare bit of optimism pushed through the crust of my mind. I risked to think that I may feel the pleasure of joy again.

The soft exhausting sand turned to hard, packed dirt. My bare feet were tender, but no longer cracked, and leaving a trail of life-giving fluids. The rhythm of pain missed several beats.

A river.

I fell on my aching knees and drank from the life-giving river with joyous abandonment. I slurped and cackled. I drooled, sputtered, and splashed. No dignity was going to stop the deepest, cool water from invigorating my body or from washing the weights from my spirit and soul. I wanted it all. I wasn't leaving that river until every grain of sand was swept away by the current, never to abrase my joy again. My senses were alive and vibrant. I had been given another chance to find myself.

As the refreshing droplets were kissed dry by the setting sun, I reflected on what I had released. My briefcase – a rock of my identity that had been exposed as an anchor. My clothes – previously, my camouflage. My perspectives and attitudes - more numerous than my physical scraps. I was unshackled from this nightmare in time and watched the welcome sunrise of another day.

Holy City

As the last of the flecks of disappointment washed from my eyes, it felt like the faint mists of the morning sun were God's breath, bathing me with mercy. I looked up.

A city of gold! How had I missed it? How had I walked so long in the Desert without seeing it?

The sun caught the wonderful image with rare perfection. The shimmering sight gleamed of hope, scattering volleys of redemption across the sky and peace into my heart. It was a sight that one could only see in the middle of the desert. A sight that was worth all the treasure in the world. A healing sight that left dreams pale in comparison.

A welcome sign hung, somehow unattached, floating in the heavens around it. I now realize it was this city of pure gold, shining in the midst of the sand, bestowing gifts of peace, hope, joy, and trust in the Divine, which gently guided me through the beating sands.

A holy city, proclaiming victory over the Desert. A city of liberation from the harsh exile of the Desert. A city with a promise of everlasting covenant of freedom from the bonds of slavery.

At once, I knew my journey through the Desert was worth it.

DESERT DEVOTIONAL

"Remember how the L<small>ORD</small> your God led you all the way in the wilderness these forty years, to humble and test you in order to know what was in your heart, whether or not you would keep His commands. He humbled you, causing you to hunger and then feeding you with manna, which neither you nor your ancestors had known, to teach you that man does not live on bread alone but on every word that comes from the mouth of the L<small>ORD</small>. Your clothes did not wear out and your feet did not swell during these forty years. Know then in your heart that as a man disciplines his son, so the L<small>ORD</small> your God disciplines you." (Deuteronomy 8:2-5 NIV)

The desert is a barren land, an undesirable place of lack, known for its hostile conditions. Yet, in the spiritual journey, it is the domain of transformation. It's a place of stripping, removing, and breaking. It's a place of testing and provision. So much happens in the desert, much of it unpleasant, but all of it formational.

This principle is clearly revealed in the pathway Yahweh fashioned for His people in response to their cry for freedom from generations of slavery.

Now, if you or I were scripting Israel's freedom story, we might have written a stereotypical rescue plot that included an unsung hero leading the underdog Israelite slaves into an impossible victory against their arch enemy, then heading straight into the Promised Land to live happily ever after. But that was not their journey, and neither is it ours.

Israel was led out of Egypt as slaves. Those slaves were led into the wilderness to be tested and transformed into a bride. That bride was then led into the Promised Land as a warrior bride. This is the path of spiritual maturity; slave to bride to warrior bride.

Yahweh chose not to take slaves into the land He promised for His bride. The Promised Land was not for a people who only knew Him as Rescuer, but for a people who knew Him also as Husband. The Promised Land was for those who had experienced and encountered the power and intimacy of His bridal love (Ephesians 5:25-27).

Before the Israelites left Egypt, they lived as slaves for more than four centuries. Not a single one of them had ever lived as a free person. They all had "slave identities." That identity metastasized into their thinking and everyday lives. In fact, it didn't take long after leaving Egypt for the degraded contents of their hearts and minds to be exposed (Exodus 32:1-14). Clearly, the people who entered the wilderness were not ready to possess, guard, thrive, and enjoy the Promised Land. They needed an extreme makeover – exchanging a slave identity for their true identity as the bride of one Husband.

The wilderness removed all means of providing for themselves creating room for Yahweh to give His people manna (Exodus 16:35, Number 11:9, Matthew 6:11). The wilderness removed all means of sourcing raw materials to making clothing and sandals, allowing room for Yahweh to temporarily breach His created order by suspending normal wear and tear of their Egyptian wardrobe for the duration of the forty-year journey (Deuteronomy 8:4). There was no slave master in the wilderness. This allowed them to freely choose to trust and follow Yahweh who revealed Himself as cloud during the day and as fire during the night (Exodus 13:21).

The wilderness experience exposed and reformatted false beliefs, ideas, and conclusions about Yahweh. Every limiting thought, every inner vow and agreement based in fear and resentment, and every guarded heart dissolved slowly as the Israelites were romanced into a place of loving their Husband with their whole hearts, whole minds, souls, and strength (Deuteronomy 6:5).

The wilderness is where the bride was purified, refined, strengthened, and empowered. The testing and resistance of the wilderness transformed the bride into a warrior bride, a reflected image of her Husband – one who obeyed without hesitation, trusted without questioning, remained faithful no matter the price, acted with an undivided heart and mind (John 14:9).

On a similar journey, Jesus was led by the Holy Spirit into the desert to be tempted for forty days (Luke 4:1-14). He not only went without food and water, but without shelter or a place to lay His head to rest. He endured the hot, hostile environment of daytime and the isolation of chilling nights. He was being prepared through battle, through testing the limits of his body, mind, and spirit. After Jesus resisted the devil and remained faithful to His Father, *"He returned to Galilee in the power of the Spirit"* to fulfil His sacred assignment (Luke 4:14 NIV).

After forty years in the wilderness, Yahweh led His warrior bride toward Jericho, to begin their sacred assignment. On the journey to Jericho, Yahweh issued a unique, if not bewildering, military strategy. "March and blow the trumpet and I will give you the city" (Joshua 6:2-5). It's unlikely a slave nation would have agreed to such a nonsensical strategy. But as a warrior bride nation, Israel agreed wholeheartedly expecting her Husband to do as He promised.

I think it's His grace that leads us to places where we have nothing to grab hold of, no defense, no excuses, nothing with which to cover up or pretend, a place of desperation where He is our all in all. It's not to shame us, but to free us, refine us, and empower us. To love the Lord your God with all your heart, soul, and strength is not only the greatest commandment, it is the most direct path to living a life of freedom and adventure.

Would you willingly choose to enter the wilderness and let Him refine you and discover Him in unique ways?

Practical Application

1. What are the places in your heart and mind where you still feel enslaved, shackled, weighed down, blocked – places you feel you need a breakthrough? Write them down. Then invite Him to show you the root; maybe a memory of something done or said by you or to you, or a limiting belief taught to you, or fear of man. Release these things and declare a kingdom agreement with His truth.
2. Is there anything in your heart or mind that causes you to hold back or hesitate? Are there places in your heart or mind where you don't know Him? Maybe places where there's fear, doubt, unbelief, disappointment, or even resentment at Him? Let Him go to those places with you and show you how He has always been with you. Let Him exchange fear for love, unbelief for faith, disappointment for trust, and resentment for forgiveness.
3. Are there things in your life that are serving as distractions, filling up time and space, and stealing opportunities to connect more with Him? Would you be willing to let Him speak to you about laying some of those things aside, maybe even some good things, to allow for more time and room to connect with Him?
4. Have you allowed what's happened to you or what you've done to serve as your identity? Would you be willing to lay all that down (Philippians 2:7), and let Him reveal to you the kingdom identity He's written on you and ask to be filled with His power to live that out?

THE JEWELLERY BOX

Link to music score:
www.jdaymusic.com

In the Beginning

Long before the heavens were created, when the swirling of the nations was a simple mist, when even the grains of sand were still just the imagination of the Father, He thought of a wonderful gift for Himself.

Love Contained

He moulded love into a container. His mighty finger cast a shadow imprinting the box as His. To prevent love from spilling out the sides, He placed a border of the purest gold around it. The moistness of his nostrils breathed intricate designs over the lid and shined every surface.

Angelic Song

Within each surface, He placed songs He collected of the angel choir. Every time He held the box, a new song would release, summoning the angel choir to harmonize in agreement. No two songs ever sounded the same. And with each song, another army of heavenly hosts was birthed, together permeating the essence of His creation.

Finest Gems

It was a box fit for the Father's most precious jewels. He would take all the time of creation to tenderly make His choices for this box.

One day as He began to breathe the world into existence, streams of endless light flowed from the first sunrise. "Aha", He whispered to His audience of angels, "Look at its splendour. I will capture a ray and squeeze it into a gem of the greatest value. I will place it in my box so I can look at it when I long for this moment of pleasure."

As centuries traveled into time and history existed, the Father captured rare moments of beauty and raw creation. Each moment was fashioned into a jewel, a history-treasure, and then purposefully placed into His precious jewellery box.

Each jewel became His favourite and it brought Him such pleasure. Some nights He simply opened the box and ran His fingers over the brightly polished and shining jewels. On occasion, He took a gem and playfully nudged an angel declaring, "Remember when We made this one, wasn't that a favoured day."

Time never caused the jewels to fade or tarnish. If anything, the more history crept through the existence of the universe, the more valuable each gem became.

The Final Jewel

One day, a particularly heart wrenching day, the Father said it was time for a new gem – one of matchless cut, color, and carat. As Father looked down on Earth from His heavenly throne, He pondered how He would contain this moment.

"Oh yes, there it is!" The perfect jewel, the one He had been waiting for. This will complete the beauty of His collection. He declared to the infinite expanse of time, "This will make the jewellery box perfect."

He reached out His loving hand and picked up a splinter from the cross, covered with the blood of His Son. He held it to His heart and released a battle cry like a mighty Lion claiming its territory and rallying stray members of the pride.

"This," He said, "is the final jewel for my box."

"This completes my favourite collection."

"It is finished!"

The Release

Then the Father gave the release order, "I've chosen the ones who will be the bearers of this jewellery box. What joy this one will bring them when they see all that I've placed inside."

Jewellery Box Devotional

"Before I formed you in the womb, I knew you, before you were born I set you apart; I appointed you as a prophet to the nations." (Jeremiah 1:5 NIV)

Just as the Father inscribed "prophet to the nations" on Jeremiah, He has written a kingdom purpose on you. Before He began knitting you in your mother's womb, it was written on you. Before you lived a single day, He had already placed personality traits, preferences and tastes, gifts, talents and abilities, desires, and dreams inside you (Psalm 139:13-18). He had already seen you fully stepping forward in your kingdom identity and into the purposes written on you. Who you are and how you are, the dreams, and desires that reside deep inside of you have all been established by the Father's declaration.

You are "on purpose."

We tend to think of our story as beginning apart from Him, therefore, needing to invite Him into our story. But the truth unveiled in Jeremiah 1:5 is that He chose for you to be here, now, in this moment in history, for a very specific purpose in His continually unfolding redemptive story. The truth is – you are in His story.

What's more, He's made advance preparation for all you require to accomplish the purposes He's written upon your life. But there is a catch. He hasn't placed inside you all that you need to fulfil your kingdom destiny. The good news is that you don't have to create those things. You're simply invited to go on a scavenger hunt and find them.

Let me explain.

We tend to think that when the Father completes the good work He has begun in us (Philippians 1:6) that it will be like Him completing a big jigsaw puzzle. We hope that once He puts all of our puzzle pieces into the right place that we'll feel complete in our understanding of whom we are and the big picture of our lives. But here's the thing.

You're a living puzzle, and as you trust Him and choose to expand the boundaries of your faith, He will keep expanding the picture of who you are and His purposes for you. His work is never complete, like we tend to think.

And, here's another thing. You don't have all the pieces to your own puzzle. Other people are pieces of your puzzle, and you are a piece of other's puzzle. None of us are actually designed to fulfil our kingdom destiny on our own. He's made it that way.

He's made us like the Trinity (Genesis 1:26). They never act independent of each other (John 3:11). They never leave or forsake one another and are never unaccompanied by an angelic host (Matthew 26:53, Revelation 5:11-12, Revelation 19:14).

In the same way, the Father has given you His Holy Spirit and assigned angels to you as the "unseen pieces" of your puzzle (Psalm 91:11, Revelation 19:10, Revelations 22:9). And He has selected other people to be the "seen pieces" of your puzzle.

Some of what He has placed in you is actually to help others fulfil their kingdom purposes. And some of what He has placed in others is actually to help you fulfil your kingdom purposes. You are invited to find out who your puzzle pieces are and build relationships with them.

This is amazing! The Father has given you His Holy Spirit to lead you into all truth, to teach you, comfort you, and empower you with boldness and wisdom in order to witness the impossible become possible with Him. Plus, He has assigned angels to strengthen and watch over you, steadying your feet, battling for you – all empowering you fulfil the words the Father has spoken over your life (Psalm 103:20). And He has carefully chosen a few precious people to walk with you, help you grow (Proverbs 27:17), support you, and come into agreement (Matthew 18:19) to help you fulfil what He's called you to do.

The kingdom of darkness is well aware of what's written on you. They are on assignment to distract, block, and blind you from perceiving your destiny. Their main objective is to lure you into compromising your identity, as they work to bring unbearable pain your way so you feel ashamed and disqualified.

But you must know this – what the Father has written on you cannot be erased. Nothing you have done, nothing that has happened to you – nothing can erase what He has written on you. Nothing can change the Father's heart or mind about you. His grace ensures that nothing has the power to overwrite what He's written on you.

So, would you be willing to relate to yourself based on what He has written on you? Jesus did.

In Revelations 19:11-16, John describes one of my favourite images of Jesus, the Word of God, riding on a white horse, wearing a white robe dipped in blood and many crowns upon His head, followed by massive armies of heaven. He described Jesus' eyes as being ablaze and a mighty sword coming from His mouth with which He judged and waged war on His enemies. John heard Him called, "Faithful and True." He also noticed a name written on Him that no one but the Father could discern. And then John saw something written on His vestige and thigh, for all to see, *"King of Kings and Lord of Lords"*(Revelation 19:16 NIV). That's what's written on Him!

Jesus has always known who He is. He relates to Himself based on what the Father has written on Him. All creation knows who He is and relates to Him as King of Kings and Lord of Lords. The principalities, powers, authorities, angels in the kingdom of Light, and the entire kingdom of darkness all know who He is (Matthew 8:29, Mark 1:24, Mark 5:7, Luke 4:34). And every knee will bow to Him by a free will choice or as an act of reverence (Isaiah 45:22-24, Romans 14:11, Philippians 2:10).

Practical Application

1. What has the Father written on you? If you're not sure or have never asked, why not ask Him?
2. Thank Him for your unseen team – Holy Spirit and angels. Welcome them to your day. Ask the Father what He is doing today and how He wants you to join Him.
3. Thank Him for the people He has chosen as pieces of your puzzle. If you don't know who they are yet, ask Holy Spirit to show and confirm to you who they are. Then ask Him what you can do to strengthen your connection with them. Take time and pray for them. Ask for an increase of the gifts and talents He's placed in them and the faith to trust and obey.

4. What gifts, talents, abilities, interests, passions, or dreams has He placed in you? What are you doing to develop and steward them? Would you be willing to take time and give Him permission to highlight an area or two that He wants to do some work on? Ask for increase in those areas.
5. Pray Joel 2:28 over yourself and those who are pieces of your puzzle. Ask Holy Spirit to release His Spirit of Prophesy in you and in them and to give you and your team kingdom dreams and visions and expect He will answer.

KEYS

Link to music score:
www.jdaymusic.com

The Preparation

The excitement mounted, second by second.

Angels prepared the building, swept it clean, and readied it for the great celebration. They planted many golden seeds, wrapped in tiny gems, resting just beneath the floorboards. Dewdrops from heaven watered them and sunshine from the brightness of His Glory called them upward.

As more heavenly hosts gathered, great anticipation grew making the leaves on the branches of the variety of trees outside bend toward the building. The birds in the air flew just a little closer, drawn by the preparations of the angelic choir. Even the busyness of the crawling creatures in the dark cracks of the building's corners took a break to watch the angels prepare for the celebration of the Master Creator. It was an atmosphere of a great celebration.

The Call

From the first note of music until the last chime of harmony, the guarding Angels took their post and the seeds that broke forth looked like a lush forest bed. The green life grew up the walls as the littlest of angels joyfully pinned the fresh, tender vines to the pillars. The musicians and the singers took their places not seeming to realize that they were walking on a carpet of spring flowers. Following them was the aroma of mountain air, crystal blue skies and powerful rock face, blended with meadows of fresh lilies and ferns.

The notes of worship blasted their way through the roof, up into the darkening evening sky where the stars memorized the songs that were sung, permanently implanting each note in the DNA of heaven.

The Arrival

Then the guests of honour arrived, each with new life on their minds. Many carried a weight of busy. Many were hungry. Most were hurt, bruised, and bleeding. Some were filthy and others were pompous. It didn't matter.

The Welcome

Jesus welcomed each one, as they were, without a request that they come cleaned up or perfect. His delight in each one was clear. He was smiling and laughter was His countenance.

Freedom

As each was greeted, lightning flashed from the throne room, severing their chains of slavery. Most didn't know chains bound them until they felt their freedom. The fallen chains disintegrated as gratitude filled the room, directed as praise to the Father, Master, and Saviour. The celebration took place just as it was orchestrated. Every detail was perfect. Not one beat out of place.

The Key

Then the scar-riddled hand of the Great I Am reached from His Place of Glory and handed each a key. A key containing liquid gold, acquired at a great cost. It was a key to the City of Gold.

The throne room's declaration "Welcome home" completed the reception.

KEYS DEVOTIONAL

"Or suppose a woman has ten silver coins and loses one. Doesn't she light a lamp, sweep the house and search carefully until she finds it? And when she finds it, she calls her friends and neighbours together and says, 'Rejoice with me; I have found my lost coin.' In the same way, I tell you, there is rejoicing in the presence of the angels of God over one sinner who repents." (Luke 15:8-10 NIV)

Have you ever hosted a surprise birthday party for someone, planned a wedding, coordinated a community or corporate event, or trained for a sporting event like a marathon? The volume of preparation is always grossly disproportionate to the duration of the actual event. Weeks or months of planning and preparing or training can be realized in a matter of minutes or hours.

The same is true in the spirit realm. Consider the salvation experience.

Many of us have a parent, grandparent, friend, son, or daughter who interceded for years for our "welcome home" encounter. Maybe there were multiple divine encounters along the way leading to the one moment that changed everything.

I believe that part of our "knowing fully" will include an unveiling of what and who was involved in our rescue from the kingdom of darkness into the kingdom of light. I have no doubt it will be one of the most humbling and grateful moments in our lives.

I've had the privilege of being a part of many such encounters. One of my favourite "welcome home" stories from childhood occurred when I was twelve, during the summer of 1978.

My dad decided to take my younger brother and I to our first Major League Baseball game in Toronto, Canada. The Blue Jays were hosting the Detroit Tigers. At the completion of nine innings, the score was tied. As the game continued deep into extra innings, I remember wishing it would all just end as the novelty was wearing off. Then, finally, in the thirteenth inning, a solo homerun by Toronto's Otto Velez ended the game, triggering a mass evacuation of the thirty thousand plus fans from Exhibition Stadium.

We started walking toward the nearest GO-train station to retrace our way to the parking lot where our Buick LaSabre awaited the two-and-a-half-hour trek back to our home in Goderich.

When we arrived at the station platform, my dad rushed into a nearby bathroom to prepare for the drive home while my brother and I sat on a bench waiting for the next train. A train arrived and had just left as my dad made his way back to us.

About halfway, he was intercepted by a man who had just stepped off the train. He seemed to know my dad, and my dad seemed to know him. After a few minutes of intense conversation, my dad informed us that we'd been invited to stay overnight at this man's house. It was very late and my brother and I were ready to crash.

It was only later that we learned "the rest of the story."

The man was a VP at the Bank of Montreal. He worked late and then attended a Neil Diamond concert at Massey Hall to avoid going home to an empty house because his wife and kids were out of town, magnifying the lingering emptiness he'd been feeling for years.

He didn't consider himself much of a person of faith, but while on the GO-train, he asked God to send help. He attended church a few times out of courtesy, while visiting relatives. The pastor of that church was the only pastor he knew by name, so he asked God to help him find a way to connect with that pastor. In fact, he had actually decided to leave the concert early to go home, hunt down the pastor's telephone number, and give him a call.

As he got off the GO-train, he was in total shock as he saw my dad walking toward him. My dad was that pastor. No doubt, you can guess how this story ends.

My dad talked to him about Jesus, the One to whom he had just prayed to on the train, the One who had been interceding for him his whole life, the One who had just arranged for the only person he believed could help him connect to God to be in his city, on that very day, at that very moment.

Consider the preparation that went into this encounter. The Father was able to take into account a delay in a baseball game and the time it would take the three of us to make our way through the crowd and walk to this man's train stop, and align the unfolding of those events with the timeline created by this man's decision to work late, attend a concert, then leave early, along with the schedule of the train he was on, in order to facilitate an otherwise impossible encounter with the only pastor he knew by name. In all, fourteen independent factors were coordinated to facilitate this man's "welcome home" celebration. All this for just one!

Can you imagine the excitement of the heavenly host and cloud of witnesses as they watched the sequence of events unfolding that night? It must be surreal to watch the Father pursue His wandering kids, step by step, day after day, while never usurping their will. The Father gently and graciously, influences and leads His lost sons and daughters into a divine collision with the ones who have already been found.

He never sleeps and never slumbers (Psalm 121:4). He is always at work (John 5:17). And He is looking for those who would be willing to work with Him and claim His full inheritance. How about you?

Practical Application

1. Thank the Father for all that He did to arrange for your "welcome home" encounter. Thank Him for everyone who was part of your rescue mission.
2. You are in His story. He has work for you to do with Him. Would you be willing to offer yourself as a co-labourer and be part someone else's "welcome home" celebration?
3. Everything happens in the Spirit first. Would you be willing to join Him in intercession for whomever He leads you to pray for? Let Him speak to you about how to pray for that person. If a name drops into your mind throughout the day, trust that it's for a reason and begin to pray for them.
4. I enjoy asking the Holy Spirit to show me a face or tell me a name of a person to look out for during the day. Would you trust Him to do that for you? Ask Him for a word picture or message to share with that person. Write it down. Keep a log. Then go and expect to be part of an impossible encounter. Keep a log of the "welcome home" stories you get to be part of and then tell the stories.

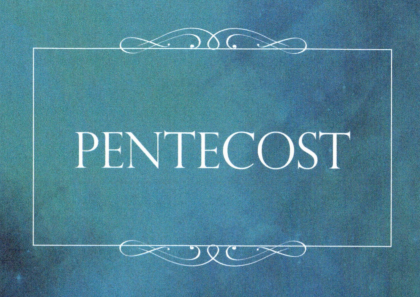

PENTECOST

Link to music score:
www.jdaymusic.com

All Things New

I am now old and my slowing body reminds me daily that I have more history than future. But my memories of the man they called Simon Peter are as fresh as the days of my youth. We called that season the days of The Great Revive.

It was a time where politics and religion were a tumultuous mix, opinions clashed, and war was ready to explode with each restless minute. It was a time of adventure and anticipation during which we witnessed firsthand the birth of the new church.

View from the Shadows

I was a nobody. A slave girl. My job was simply to obey the demands of the gatekeeper and to open the gate to the courtyard. The gate was large and made of steel bars, ten times wider and heavier than I was. Opening it was a large task for such a small girl. It took strength that I did not have and I received many beatings for my weakness. However, it was a task that allowed me to hide in the shadows of the great visitors and silently share in the conversations of the scholars.

I would play games in the shadow of the great gate, games of invisibility and freedom from my long days of standing. I could learn and form opinions with no criticism or judgment because I was invisible to the sophisticated crowd. I heard the words that were directed only to the chosen few. I was not a chosen one, but the naivety of youth resisted the culling of my curiosity and I heard the secrets of the season.

I watched. I heard. I held secrets.

The Garden Remembered

There was a dark stirring in the atmosphere on the night that my cousin, Malchus, lost his ear by sword. He told me an intoxicating story of yelling and the suddenness of the sword that was so close to severing his life from this world, but only severed his ear. He told me about the excruciating pain and the Man who turned his blood to liquid love. He told me how the Man the soldiers were apprehending placed His hand on his ear and it was healed immediately. He talked about the Man's eyes and how He saw deep into Malchus' fears. He said he felt a rush of warmth that started in his heart and pumped the troubles of his youth away. Malchus spoke of love and acceptance, words that my tender heart longed for.

Strange things had happened that night, but stranger things were yet to come.

Inner Conflict

During the days before the great Feast, I remember seeing the man they called Simon Peter. He was loud, aggressive, and so compelling. I noticed how he walked with an edge of arrogance through the streets of our dusty town. I wanted to despise the truth he carried, as I could see that it threatened the Elders of our community. It rubbed the holy men the wrong way and it clashed with what I found secure. I wanted to tell him to leave our town and to stop unravelling our years of secure teaching.

Yet I wanted him to stay. When he would speak, he drew purpose out of me and I longed to know more. It was more than a common slave girl could ever dream of. But dreams grow. Dreams can't be held back when the dream is to know the Creator, the Maker of Life.

I saw that same dream in the hope Peter carried. I yearned to know more. I was eager to listen to his rendition of life. I desired something that I thought only the Jewish men were privileged to hear.

I watched. I heard. I held secrets.

The Denial

The night of the Great Sorrow was the only time I ever spoke to Simon Peter. He came through the gate on my watch. Fear was seeping from his eyes. Terror and confusion could not be hidden that night. I could tell that he longed to draw closer to see the Man they called The Christ.

I moved from my covering, nearer to where he stood, and asked him, "Are you not one of them?" He quietly said, "No." The denial of his words could not cover the love in his heart. But as he spoke the denial, I could feel daggers of pain like fragments of a broken glass penetrating the deepest parts of Simon Peter's heart. He was on the edge of fleeing, but his desire to see the Man kept him in the courtyard.

As he stood by the fire-filled barrel, I could see the flames light up his face and mockingly lick at the pain in his eyes. I could tell the sorrow that came from him was more than most men could handle. It was an internal war that could find no victory.

He was asked again, and then again, "Are you not one of them?" More denial, more pain. I could see agony bleed from his heart and the terror in his eyes turned to defeat. His arrogant nature was broken. The hope that was once in his heart was bruised. I wanted to scold him for turning on his friend, but the brokenness of his heart was penance enough.

Then, in the earliest of light, when the sun only jokes to relieve the darkness, the birds began to shatter the silence. I saw it happen. His eyes met the eyes of The Christ. It was as fast as a lightning strike. It caused Simon Peter's knees to buckle from the weight of the denial. It was the first time I saw Simon Peter for what he really was – just a man.

Confessions in the Shadow

Many dark days followed the night of the Great Sorrow. Death and hopelessness marked that time. Mysteries and secrets became our normal language. All the while, I was ever protected by the shadows of the gate.

One day, I remember hearing Simon Peter lamenting to the Secret Ones. It was a cool spring afternoon. The sun was just about to meet the land. I was hiding behind the huge steel gate and heard him confess the stories that crushed his hope.

He recalled the days when he thought victory was his right. Now, he spoke as a man who had lost his greatest strength – his faith. He spoke with a voice of defeat. I had to draw closer to hear. I was careful to not expose my hiding place. I risked being caught, but I needed to hear. I longed to learn more of the secrets of the season.

The Watching

For fifty days, I secretly watched Simon Peter. I quietly followed him, studying the pattern of his pain. Peter was not the arrogant man that I once saw walk into the courtyard. He was broken, yet I wanted what he had. He had been with the King.

I watched. I heard. I held secrets.

The Waiting

Simon Peter and the Secret Ones started gathering daily in the upper room of a house given to them by the ones that believed. It was an empty room, but I could sense the destiny of the room. The clay bricks had a story already scribed on the mortar. Every day, the room was filled with people. I never let them see me watching, longing, and hoping to be invited into the room. Somehow I felt that it was not for me. After all, I was only a slave girl.

But I watched. I heard. I held secrets.

The Fire

Then, one night I dreamt of fire and freedom. As the next morning arrived, I knew, after all the waiting and watching, that the time had come. I wasn't exactly sure what I was to watch or listen for, but I knew something was about to change.

I was not supposed to be in that house. But I found a hiding place in the darkest corner by the shadows. Then the fire saw me. I was not left out.

At first I felt the prickle of anticipation beat in my chest. Then it rose to my ears and then soon I was aware of the fire that Simon Peter said the Christ had spoken of. I could see it with my eyes. I could feel the heat on my skin. I saw the movement of a small flicker. It was a ball of fire skipping, turning, and rotating with a blue heat and yellow glow. It was dancing! Growing! Bouncing along the heads of the children, passing from generation to generation!

I saw it! Me, a slave girl!

The fire was ever growing. It enveloped every fold and cavity of each heart. The fire consumed our communion, pushing its way past doubt, fear, and failure.

Then I then saw the Angel army escorting fireballs from the throne room and casting crowns on each bowed head of the waiting crowd. The fire was alive, saturated with the awe of our Creator. It was extreme and all consuming, brimming with love and mercy on a grander scale than creation.

Somehow the dust of doubt and the dirt of wounds were being burned to a char and the residue became a dusting of gold mirrored on every face. We were given freedom to brush off the ashes and see the gems that had replaced our iniquities. I felt an intense power surge within me. I was consumed by a loving fear that drove every demon to its screeching knees.

New Tongues

I tried to stand, but being covered with the shroud of this unknown glory made my knees resistant to venturing away from the peace of the Holy Ground. I remember trying to open my mouth and hearing the trumpet sound of angels. Then, a symphony of sounds flooded from my belly out of my mouth, and to the sky.

I heard the release of Holy Power come from my mouth – words I could not describe then and cannot describe now. Sounds I had never heard spoken at the gate. It was a language of love, a language of war.

I was reading a script that was scribed in heaven by the Father's own hand. My words joined with the others to declare the magnitude of the Messiah.

Fresh Wind

Accompanying the fire was a strange new wind. It caressed our bodies in a torrent of power, passing the strength of an army, but as gentle as the summer breeze. The wind whipped through with tornado force, but hardly moved a hair on my head. It was a contrast of strength and hope. It brought the fresh smell of spring rising across a mountain range and pomegranate blossoms mixed with fig vines. It was a current of life and hope blended with power and unearthly strength.

Out of the Shadows

Once the fire and wind passed by, our words became cheers, then whispers. I didn't care who heard me. For the first time since the night of Great Sorrow, I was not hiding. I didn't care who saw me.

New Birth

We all began to see the emerging birth of a Church as we had never seen it before. A Church made from the molecular bonding of God to mankind, a Church without the confines of rules, but existing on the truth of His love and power. I heard words such as "love" and "acceptance."

We were given a new mandate to spread the news and not to hide in the shadows. We heard that we were worthy of His love. He said to speak of the secrets that were shown.

No Longer a Slave

I finally understood what I had been yearning for. I knew His secrets.

I never saw Simon Peter after the Day of Power, but I no longer needed to live through his experiences. I had finally met the one called the Christ. My searching ended with greater power and more answers than any mere human could give me.

I know I have a mere few days left in this world, but my life has been rich – richer than I could ever have asked or imagined.

I've watched. I've heard. I've shared His secrets.

PENTECOST DEVOTIONAL

"Then Peter stood up with the Eleven, raised his voice and addressed the crowd." (Acts 2:14 NIV)

"When they saw the courage of Peter and John and realized that they were unschooled, ordinary men, they were astonished and they took note that these men had been with Jesus." (Acts 4:13 NIV)

It was undeniable. Peter had changed. Clearly, this was not the same person who crumbled under questioning regarding his association to Jesus. He was bold and speaking with an authority not acquired through traditional means.

So what happened to Peter?

Acts 2:1-4 details how those in the upper room heard the sound of violent winds, saw tongues of fire resting over each other's heads, and were in awe as they heard their friends speaking in foreign languages. All this, while the multinational crowd passing by was understandably dumbfounded at hearing local Jews declaring the wonders of God in their native tongues. The whole scene was surreal and unprecedented.

Since that day, there has been much discussion about a possible explanation for the sound of the rushing wind, and there has been plenty divisive debate about speaking in tongues.

But have you ever wondered why there were tongues of fire? What were they a sign of? Were they simply meant as a visual confirmation that they were indeed being baptized in the Holy Spirit and fire as they spoke in tongues? Or is it possible there might have been something more going on?

There's a saying, "It matters where you start and stop a story." And to wade into this question, I want to start this story at Peter's infamous three-part denial of Jesus.

While Peter might have been the lead character thrust to center stage by the gospel writers, he wasn't the only one who abandoned Jesus. By the time Peter's third denial triggered the rooster's crow, all Twelve were on the run. They all bore the weight of denial in what was a dramatic transition from a beautiful act of unity, breaking bread together, just a few hours earlier, to breaking rank and loyalty to the One they declared to be their Messiah.

Given their modus operatus of waiting for an opportune time (Luke 4:13), I can only imagine the strength of the coordinated attack unleashed by the kingdom of darkness against the disciples, and especially Peter. Their ruler knew well the destiny written on Peter, *"On this rock, I will build my church and the gates of Hades will not prevail against it"* (Matthew 16:18 NIV). This had to be, without a doubt, Satan's best opportunity to destroy the ones through whom Jesus promised to launch His post-resurrection Church. This was it, the attempted sifting of Peter, for which Jesus warned and interceded (Luke 22:31). The torment and shame from the accuser of the brethren must have been unequalled.

Consider Peter's record and what was in the accuser's arsenal.

Peter was used by Satan to tempt Jesus from His messianic mission, which led to an unforgettable rebuke by Jesus, *"Get behind me Satan."* (Matthew 16:23 NIV). He declared his unwavering loyalty to Jesus, even to the death, only to deny Him a short time later (Mathew 26:35). He fell asleep, three times, in the Garden of Gethsemane, along with two other of Jesus' chosen intercessors, during one of Jesus' most challenging moments prior to enduring the suffering of the cross (Matthew 26:36-46). And during Jesus' arrest, he fell prey to darkness again impulsively cutting off the ear of one of the centurions leading to yet another rebuke from Jesus (John 18:10-11). Then of course, there were the three denials punctuated by the sound of a rooster crowing (Matthew 26:69-75).

There can be no doubt that these forced remembrances of Peter's failures would have felt like prickly spines of a crown of thorns pressing against his mind, sending shrieks of pain and shame throughout his body.

Jesus allowed a crown of thorns to be placed on His head.

Although it was clearly intended by those who crucified Him to be a mocking crown of display, I think it was also a physical manifestation of the sharp, prickly, cutting thoughts that darkness was trying to wrap around His mind and tries to wrap around ours.

Consider this.

The crown of thorns they placed on Him was made from thorns taken from the earth, and then twisted into a crown by the hands of men, men under the rule and influence of the kingdom of darkness. The crown of thorns symbolized the true nature of the kingdom of darkness – dead, lifeless, twisted, sharp, painful, mocking.

Those that put the crown of thorns on Jesus considered it a display of their authority and rule over Him and His mind. But, in fact, He humbled Himself and willingly took the crown upon Himself to demonstrate that nothing of the earth or the created order, nothing man-made, and nothing from the kingdom of darkness has authority over Him. In His death, He conquered the power of death and hell. He rose with the keys of authority over sin and death. With a new crown, He rose. A Crown of Peace.

His resurrection established that darkness does not have authority or dominion over Him or His mind, which means, darkness doesn't have authority or dominion over us or our mind!

He took upon Himself the crown of thorns to destroy it, in order to demonstrate His authority over all things and selflessly give us His Crown of Peace. I think this is one of the hidden mysteries of the Pentecost story.

Consider this.

He could have placed tongues of fire in the hands or hearts of those gathered in the Upper Room. But He chose to place tongues of fire over their heads to burn every earth-bound, sharp, painful, shaming, condemning, tormenting, twisted, limiting, powerless, mocking, taunting, and disqualifying thought thrust upon their minds by the kingdom of darkness. And in exchange, each received a His Crown of Peace, confirming their kingdom identity, purpose, and authority.

He gave them His crown! And He filled each one with His fire so they could "go" and be living evidence of the Power of the Cross and burn off the thorny crowns of others.

I also think the tongues of fire were a manifestation of the fulfilment of the kingdom exchange promised in the book Isaiah, of which Jesus quoted in reference to Himself (Luke 4:18-19).

> *"The Spirit of the Sovereign LORD is on me, because the LORD has anointed me to proclaim good news to the poor. He has sent me to bind up the broken-hearted, to proclaim freedom for the captives, and release from darkness for the prisoners, to proclaim the year of the LORD's favour and the day of vengeance of our God, to comfort all who mourn, and provide for those who grieve in Zion – to* **bestow on them a crown of beauty instead of ashes**, *the oil of joy instead of mourning, and a garment of praise instead of a spirit of despair. They will be called oaks of righteousness, a planting of the LORD for the display of his splendour." (Isaiah 61:1-3 NIV)*

The Holy Spirit not only came to empower the disciples, but to free their minds from the rule of the Prince of the Air. In doing so, the disciples were freed to walk under the rule of the Prince of Peace, clearly seeing, hearing, and perceiving - advancing His kingdom on earth.

I think there's even more for us in the Upper Room story. I think it holds an important invitation and promise for us.

When the Holy Spirit came, the thin veil between the seen and unseen realm was pulled back, and the spiritual eyes of everyone in the upper room were activated, allowing them to witness the work of the All-Consuming Fire (Hebrews 12:29). They were allowed to "see" as Jesus saw.

Consider this.

Jesus said, *"The Son can do nothing by Himself; He can only do what He sees His Father doing"* (John 5:19 NIV). I think the tongues of fire were not only a visual confirmation of the coming of the promised Holy Spirit, but an actual observation of what the Father was doing – burning crowns of thorns! He fulfilled the promise of Joel 2:28 – "I will pour out my Spirit and…they will see visions!" They had been seeking Him for ten days and He not only came as He promised, but activated their spiritual eyes to observe what He instructed His Holy Spirit to do.

How amazing would it be to have your spiritual eyes opened so you could see the sharp, prickly, tormenting thoughts pressing against someone's mind? How amazing would it be to agree with the Holy Spirit to release His Fire to burn those lies and accusations and fan into flame His Fire in them?

How amazing would it be to have your spiritual ears opened to hear what the Holy Spirit desires for that person as their "Isaiah 61 exchange" and declare that over them? How amazing would it be to see the fire of faith stirring in another's heart and confidently declare what they are believing for and see it come to pass (Acts 14:8-10)?

What could possibly keep you and I from seeking after Him to "see" more, "hear" more and "perceive" more of what Jesus and the Father are doing so we can join them in fulfilling the Father's will *"on earth as it is in heaven."*

> *"You will find Me, when you seek Me with all your heart." (Jeremiah 29:13 NIV)*

Practical Application

1. Are there any sharp, prickly thoughts pressing against your mind that you need burned in His fire? Thoughts that have had a stronghold on you? Would you be willing to wait in His presence and let His Fire come and burn all that He desires to burn off your mind? Would you be willing to agree with Him and forgive the ones who seeded some of those thoughts?
2. Are you living in the shadows? Is the fear of man (reputation in the eyes of others) holding you back from living in the open? If so, would you be willing to invite the Holy Spirit to fill you with His love-fire and burn away the thorns of the fear of man? Ask Him to increase the love and fear of the Lord in you.
3. How strong is the Holy Spirit's fire inside you? Is it just a flicker, dull, strong or raging? Is there anything in your life that is dulling and dimming the fire in you? If so, would you be willing to repent and let it go? Then take time and ask the Holy Spirit to increase His fire in you.
4. Do you want to see, hear, and perceive more? Ask to be filled with the Holy Spirit and His fire. Stand in faith and declare, "*I see because He has opened my eyes to see as Jesus saw, I hear because He has opened my ears to hear as Jesus heard, I perceive because He has awakened me to perceive as Jesus did.*" Now, go and walk as Jesus walked (1 John 2:6).

CPSIA information can be obtained
at www.ICGtesting.com
Printed in the USA
LVOW06s0024310317
529102LV00009B/17/P